MY BODY, MY RULES

THIS BOOK BELONGS TO:

T0371149

For Stu, Amelie, Lulu and Freddie, with love – N.G.

For Kylie, Shona, and all my little and not so little friends at NCC – D.R.

Published in the UK by Scholastic, 2024
1 London Bridge, London, SE1 9BG
Scholastic Ireland, 89E Lagan Road, Dublin Industrial Estate, Glasnevin, Dublin, D11 HP5F

SCHOLASTIC and associated logos are trademarks and/or
registered trademarks of Scholastic Inc.

First published in Australia by Scholastic Australia, 2023

Text © Nicki Esler Gill, 2023
Illustrations © Dasha Riley, 2023

The right of Nicki Esler Gill and Dasha Riley to be identified
as the author and illustrator of this work has been asserted by them under the Copyright, Designs and Patents Act 1988.

ISBN 978 0702 33765 9

A CIP catalogue record for this book is available from the British Library.

All rights reserved.
This book is sold subject to the condition that it shall not, by way of trade or otherwise, be lent, hired out or otherwise
circulated in any form of binding or cover other than that in which it is published. No part of this publication may be
reproduced, stored in a retrieval system, or transmitted in any form or by any other means (electronic, mechanical,
photocopying, recording or otherwise) without prior written permission of Scholastic Limited.

Printed in China
Paper made from wood grown in sustainable forests and other controlled sources.

1 3 5 7 9 10 8 6 4 2

This is a work of fiction. Names, characters, places, incidents and dialogues are products of the author's imagination
or are used fictitiously. Any resemblance to actual people, living or dead, events or locales is entirely coincidental.

www.scholastic.co.uk

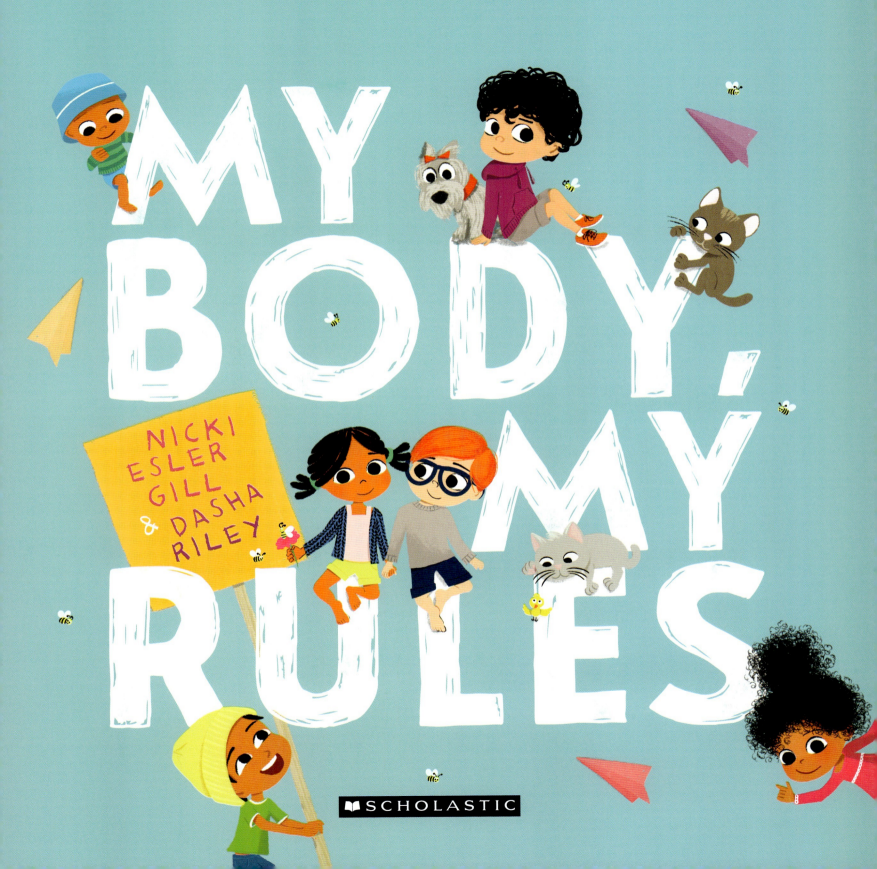

MY BODY, MY RULES

NICKI ESLER GILL & DASHA RILEY

SCHOLASTIC

Have you ever had a **cuddle**
with somebody you **love?**

Have you ridden up on shoulders
like a **giant high above?**

Have you had a **whizzy-dizzy**
with the world all spinning round?

Or received a
tummy tickle,
laughing, tumbling
on the ground?

Have you **backflipped** like a ninja

and then blocked your friend's **high-kick?**

Have you **crawled** up onto Daddy's
lap because you're feeling sick?

Have you **twirled** and **danced** and **shimmied**,
holding hands across the floor?

Or **wrapped** yourself around Mum's
leg as she walks out the door?

Have you **brushed** somebody's **hair?**
Had an aunty **pinch** your **cheeks?**

Have you **wrestled** with a cousin
till you're too worn out to speak?

Have you tied one leg together
to another person's trousers,

and won a race with three legs,
then done a **victory dance?**

But three-legged running doesn't
work if just one person's keen.

You're both sure to **face-plant**
unless working as a **team.**

One-sided **whizzy-dizzies** almost always go **awry**,
if the person being forced **lets go**,
they'll see their partner f l y.

And tickling someone who says **"No!"**
can leave them in distress

with hurt feelings and sore tummies,
so be sure they've told you

"Yes!"

And it's the same with **everything,** with hugs and kisses too.

They're not something that someone else should ever do to you,

unless they're something you would like,
and you have **told them this**

with your words, or shown with actions
that you would like a kiss.

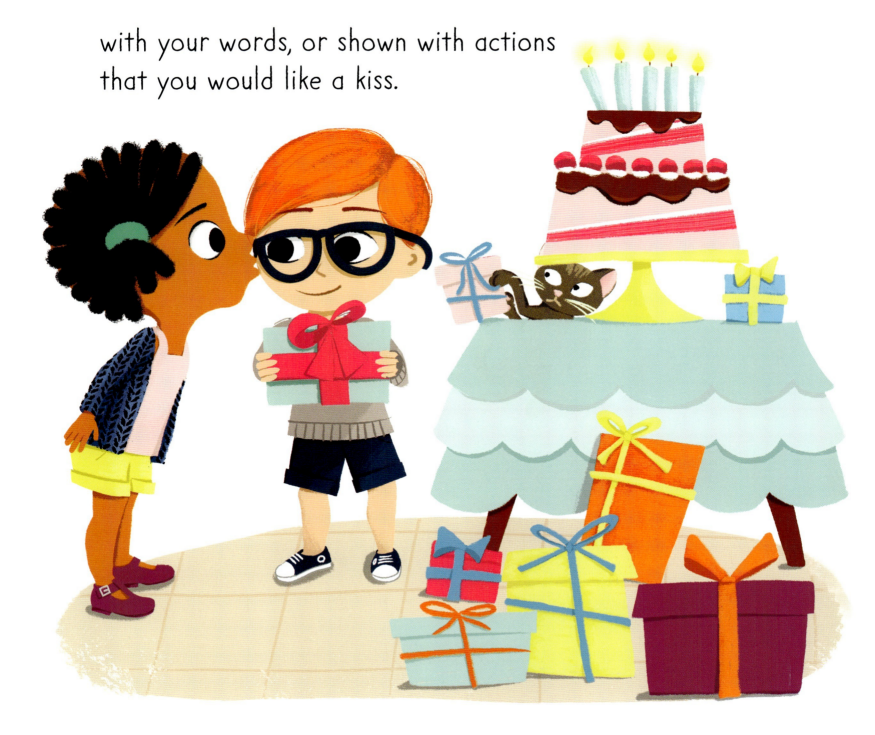

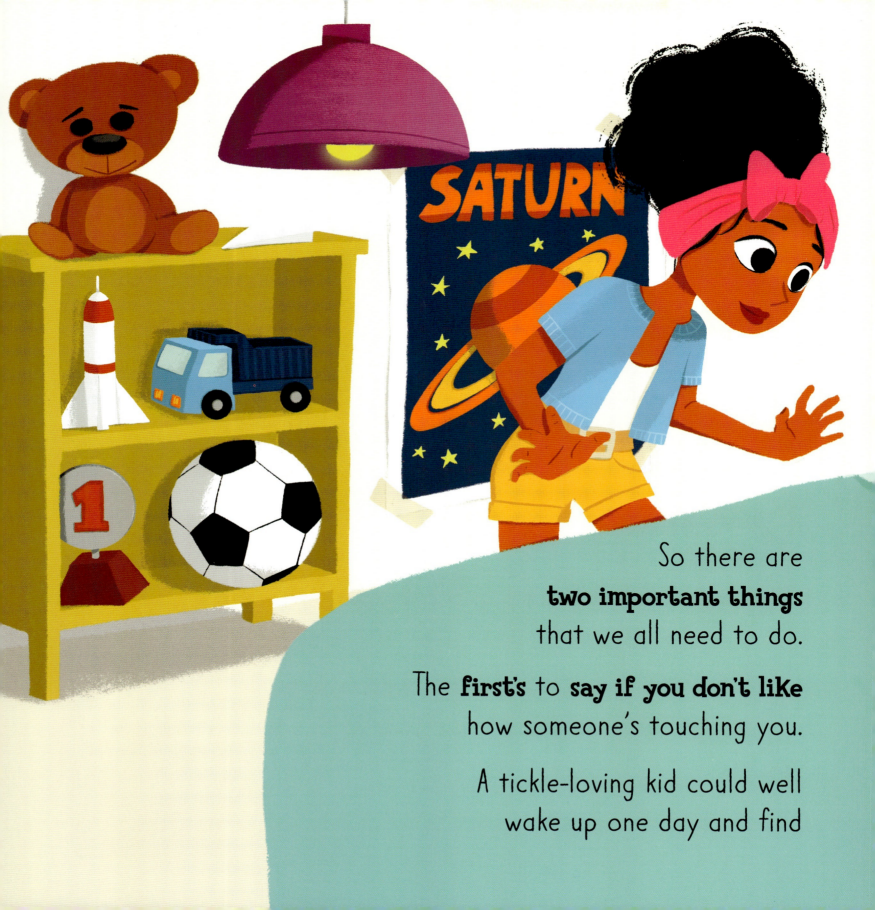

So there are
two important things
that we all need to do.

The **first's** to **say if you don't like**
how someone's touching you.

A tickle-loving kid could well
wake up one day and find

they don't like
tickles anymore –

**it's fine to change
your mind.**

Or maybe they like tickles just from **Mum** and **Dad** and **Gran,**

but **say no** to tickles coming from Aunt Jean or Uncle Stan.

And that's okay as well.

Yes, anyone's **allowed** to **say**
who they want to **tickle** them,

and **when,**
and **in what way.**

The **second** thing you need to do
is **look and listen** too,

and **learn** how someone **feels**
about a touch coming from you.

If someone says **"enough now"**
then the touching **has to end.**

It's not that they don't love you
or don't want to be your friend.

And when you're looking,
think of **cats**,
who in their catty way

will **show** that they don't
like a touch and
want to **get away**.

That's different from
a snuggly, cuddly,
happy ball of fur

who will **show** it's keen for **cuddles,**
and tell you with a purr.

A person's just the same —
I'll be sure to let you see

with my **face and actions** if I
don't want someone touching me.

But oftentimes, friends do want touch
and you can see this too,

with happy smiles and open arms,
they love to be with you.